JESUS HAD

A
BEARD

the Manly High School Man's
Guide to Manliness

CASEY NOCE

SUPERNATURAL TRUTH PRODUCTIONS, LLC
Practical Training for Spirit-Filled Living
www.SupernaturalTruth.com

ISBN: 0-9988171-0-4
ISBN-13: 978-0-9988171-0-1

Dedication

I dedicate this book to the many men of God in my life
who have mentored me and motivated me to become a
man of God myself. You have molded me as a believer,
pastor, teacher, athlete, artist, writer, and leader.

Thank you, Dad, my grandpas, my uncles, Ken, Brian,
Damon, Brooks, Art, Rick, Steven, Kyle, Zach, Josh, Jesse,
James, Eric, Daniel, Ben, and Mike.

I know that's a lot of people to dedicate a book to,
but I did it anyway.

(…and to my mom… so I don't hurt her feelings…
plus, you know, the whole birth thing.)
Love you, Mom!

Acknowledgement

I want to convey a special thanks to my *Jesus Had a Beard* class at Lenawee Christian School. I couldn't have finished this book without you Love you guys!

JESUS HAD A BEARD 🜚 — CASEY NOCE

Endorsements:

Culture is constantly trying to define how a man should act, live, respond and become successful, while neglecting the foundational truths of what makes a man of character. *Jesus Had a Beard* is the perfect guide to help any high school guy in his transition into a young man of integrity. Becoming a manly man is serious business, but it does not happen without a few chuckles. Pastor Casey's convictions through his own journey to manhood and his mentorship to many youth are interwoven throughout the entire book. This study gives a fresh look at the life of Jesus and sets a compelling example to those who are in their beginning stages of growing some stubble on their chins.

Steven Hlatky
Pastor of Outreach & Missions
Uniontown Free Methodist Church

Casey Noce has touched on an important topic for men of all ages. I have known Casey to be a man of these character traits and full of heart for Jesus after having him serve with us at the International Christian Fellowship in Rome, Italy. Combining character with the compelling scriptures in the Word of God, Casey has given men a guideline to success for relationships both personally and professionally. May we all be men like Jesus.

Rick Pasquale
Senior Pastor
International Christian Fellowship, Rome, Italy

Jesus Had a Beard is a fun, insightful read. Casey Noce has been able to take deep theology and break it down with good examples, stories, and quips, making it understandable for nearly all ages.

Tom Roy
President of Unlimited Potential, Inc.

Casey Noce has written an entertaining, Gospel-centered book that clearly reveals his heart's desire to persuade young men to think. *Jesus Had a Beard* plainly and lightheartedly uncovers that we are so flawed and defective that Jesus had to die for us. Yet we are so treasured, accepted and loved that He did so willingly and voluntarily. Ultimately, by God's grace, this produces humility, confidence, and strength. This is a smart book by one of the best young writers of the moment.

Jim "Skip" Essian
Former Chicago Cubs Manager

It would be easy to excuse *Jesus Had a Beard* as another trendy marketing scheme to sell books. For those of us who know Casey Noce and have seen "behind the curtain," nothing could be further from the truth! This is an author who practices what he preaches. Whether he's on the clock or not, he continually and consistently invests in young people and challenges the next generation of young men to embrace their destiny and calling. In addition, he has heard the cry of a fatherless and under-challenged generation and has responded in a way that is godly, honorable, and creative.

Josh Welborn
District Student Ministries Director
Assemblies of God, Michigan District

From the Editor:

Casey Noce is one of everybody's favorite people. I know few who display the joy of Jesus on such a consistent basis. Casey is also a distinctively hairy man. I truly appreciate anyone who wants to look like Jesus in both his actions and his grooming.

Casey's book is a lighthearted and enjoyable read, but it also covers some of the most important topics in any man's life. Enjoy his humor, but listen to his heart. You may not be a hairy mess like Casey, but you're definitely designed to look like Jesus in your lifestyle.

I pray God does awesome things in your life as you walk through this book.

Art Thomas
Supernatural Truth Productions, LLC
www.SupernaturalTruth.com

JESUS ʜᴀᴅ ᴀ BEARD ◖ — CASEY NOCE

Table of Contents:

Foreword

By Jeff Grenell

When young men look at older men they think a lot of things. They may think about how tall they are, how strong they are, and quite often how possible it is to be like them. What we need more of is older men who are willing to actually *be* the "Icon" these young men are seeing—or seeking. You may only be in high school right now, but you can already be an Icon to someone who looks up to you (and you probably already are).

Being an Icon means being an example in how we walk—being a mentor in how we talk. It is to be a Yoda in how we think. In these pages you will find practical ways to be an Icon, an example, a mentor, and a Yoda to the younger generation looking for help on how to become a man.

If we are going to raise young boys to become men, the concepts covered in these pages are part of the development. Each chapter has a very real trait or characteristic that is vital to spiritual maturity.

Casey has been working with young people like you and understands your world. In *Jesus Had A Beard* he has laid out a simple framework for stepping into and continuing in manhood. I have often said that the Church must learn how to turn Princes and Princesses into Kings and Queens. I think this book should be a part of that process. As you read, may you be encouraged in the traits you've already developed, and may you be challenged to step into new things that give the next generation an example worth following.

Jeff Grenell
ythology.com — Youth Leadership Coaching Network

Preface

Growing a beard is not easy. In order to open the gate to a lusciously full beard, you must obtain the three keys to growing a beard. Without these three keys, a manly beard will be just outside of your reach.

The first key is **Maturity**.

Though maturity comes with age, it is also established by experience—both firsthand and secondhand. No child can grow a beard. Growing a beard is an honor given by God to a man who has come of age. Coming of age is a phenomenon that happens to all men at one time or another. (Who is to say when a boy becomes a man?)

Regardless of the age this switch from boyhood to manhood happens, one thing is certain: a man is mature. A man is no longer naïve or closed to the truth of the world. A man understands the culture and the times he lives in, all while fighting to maintain his God-given individuality and purity, and thereby establishing the Kingdom of Heaven's dominion in the world.

The second key is **Maintenance**.

Maintenance is the repeated process of caring for your beard. If you let it grow like a weed, you will look like a dirty bum or a creepy guy with a trash-stache.

However, if you allow it to grow and maintain it with gentle strokes of tender love and fine beard oils, you will soon have on your hands a beard worthy to warm your chin. You cannot expect to have an admirable beard without focus, commitment, and discipline—all of which fall into the category of maintenance.

The third and final key to growing a manly beard is **Grace**.

A beard is a gift from God. It is a symbol of manly wisdom. If God had not designed your body to grow a beard, you would not be able to grow a beard no matter how mature you were or how much you worked at it.

Beards are given by grace. We can't grow a beard unless we have been given the ability to grow a beard. Understanding the grace by which we live and move and have our beards is foundational to growing a manly beard.

With these three keys, you will be able to grow a wonderfully manly beard.

I hope you were able to catch the spiritual undertone of the three keys to growing a beard. A beard, at least in this book, represents our relationship with God.

In order to grow in your relationship with God, you must grow in **maturity**. We grow in maturity through experiencing God in the Scriptures, other believers, and personal encounters with Him. There is something to be said about trusting someone who has already gone through what you are going through. It's wisdom. Maturity looks a lot like wisdom. A mature man doesn't wait to make his own mistakes. A mature man seeks out advice of older men so that he won't repeat the same mistakes they made. There are plenty of mistakes out there that are just waiting for you to claim as your own. Don't waste your time repeating another person's mistakes.

A relationship with God must be **well maintained**.

You cannot expect to have a strong relationship with God if you never do anything with Him. Pray, read your Bible, talk with other believers, go to church, give to missions, and serve people! Being a man of God takes commitment. I couldn't think of anything more worthy of my life's commitment than a relationship with God. Think about your relationship with your best friend. Do you spend time together? Do you laugh together? Do you go on adventures together? Do you go through difficult times together? Relationships take time and commitment. Maintaining a relationship with God looks a lot like spending time with Him.

The last key is **grace**. In order to truly have a relationship with God or truly live like Jesus, we must understand grace. We aren't able to have a relationship with God outside of grace, neither can we live as He desires. Without grace, we are separate from God and outside the empowering and enabling influence of relationship with Him.

God has given all of mankind a gift of grace which is accessible through faith (See Ephesians 2:8). He has made a way—through Jesus—to have a relationship with Him and be transformed to reveal Him in the world.

If we believe our relationship with God is based off of our maintenance or maturity, we are deceived. It is only God's goodness and faithfulness that make it possible to engage in relationship with Him, not the other way around.

All three keys open the gate to a strong relationship with God: Maturity, Maintenance, and Grace.

In the following pages, I'll teach you about eleven attributes of Jesus' manliness. **You can't produce these in your life through mere human effort.** Jesus said in John 15:5, "…apart from Me you can do nothing." Trust Jesus to produce these things in you, and then maintain them as you mature in Him

Introduction

High school is tough. It always has been. Our grandparents will always tell us stories about how they used to walk through the snow, a mile uphill, both ways, with no shoes on. Though I will never really understand how that is possible, it goes to show that even back then, high school was tough.

High school is a place where you struggle to find yourself in what seems at the time to be an endless sea of people and assignments. High School is the place and time where boys become men.

Or at least they should…

How does a boy become a man? Where do we learn what it means to be a man?

I would like to propose the idea that we learn what manliness is through people we consider to be men. Throughout history, men have set examples of what it means to be masculine.

Many men have come and gone, but one remains the shining example of manliness above all others…

Me.

That's right, me! I am the manliest of all. Admire my facial hair that grows as thick as the rainforest. Covet my stern chest hair that rises behind my Double Windsor Knot just as the sun rises over the Atlantic. Gaze at my biceps that are as massive as the Rocky Mountains.

Are you laughing yet?

No? Really?

I thought that was pretty funny. To be honest, I don't think it will get much funnier going forward.[1]

---

1 - "funnier"… Is that a word? Off to a strong start, I guess! … I digress.

The truth is, I am not the manliest man of all time. I'm not even close, although I am working toward becoming *like* the manliest man in all of human history. This man didn't necessarily exemplify all the attributes that our culture might consider "manly." However, He did give us a flawless example of how to be a man—and not just any man, a man *of God*.

This man is—drum-roll please...

Yes, you've probably already guessed the guy I'm going to talk about. After all, His name is in the title of the book—not to mention, I've capitalized the "H" in Him, He, and His. These should be sufficient clues to the inquisitive context reader.

Yes, it is Jesus! The Man. The Macho Man. The Son of God. The King of Crash. The Great Bambino!

Wait... The last two are Babe Ruth.[2] Oh, that's right—the King of kings, Lord of lords, Savior of the World, The Messiah: Jesus of Nazareth!

* Insert Fanfare Here *

This book is going to focus on the manliness of Jesus and will reveal truths that will empower your walk of

---

2 - *Sandlot* reference. Sorry if that reinforces how old you think I am.

faith with God. We will explore eleven manly attributes I believe are critical for you, the Manly High School Man, to know as you step into Christ-like manhood.

We'll cover humility, work ethic, courage, wisdom, gentleness, confidence, strength, joy, compassion, power, and love.

Are you ready to begin?

> *…o'er the laaaand of the freeeeeeeeee. And the hooooome of the BRAAAAAVE!*
>
> *PLAY BALL!*

HUMILITY
1

"Pride makes us artificial,
and humility makes us real."
~ Thomas Merton ~

It was my first mission trip ever. I found myself laying under the stars in the Blue Mountains of Jamaica. We were working at a children's home, building a retaining wall for their school and leading a vacation bible school for the kids.

I was my typical egotistical self, gaining as much

attention as I could and really enjoying the time I was having being loved by the kids there. Now, you wouldn't know I was "all about me" because I put on a pretty good show. Still, my motives were focused almost entirely on myself.

That night, we had a prayer meeting. As I prayed, I felt like I was missing something. Maybe a better way of phrasing that is I felt like it was time to grow into the man God wanted me to be. I knew I was holding on to something. I said these words, and they changed my life: "God, what do You want me to give up?" I sat there and waited for the answer.

Almost immediately after I uttered that prayer, I felt my youth pastor's hand on my shoulder. He walked me to a spot where we could talk privately. The first words out of his mouth were, "God wants you to give up…" I was all ears. I knew God was going to answer the prayer I just prayed. He continued, "God wants you to give up your SELFISH AMBITION."

I broke down and cried. I decided that moment I was truly going to live for God, regardless of the benefits I received from it. It didn't matter if it cost me everything—I was going after Jesus. I needed to humble myself and give in to God's will rather than doing all the right things for myself. I realized I could go my entire life doing good and making a name for myself without God's help. But, in the end it would all be meaningless. I humbled myself to live for God.

The next week, I began volunteering in the Kid's Ministry at our church. I didn't know at the time that it would later become my profession.

Humility doesn't devalue us; it elevates the importance of others. Jesus didn't have my youth pastor tell me that I was a no-good, prideful jerk! He lovingly told me what I needed to get rid of in my heart. I wasn't devalued; I was challenged to live up to a higher value.

This experience led me down the road of humility.

In addition, the "humble pie" I was eating after that trip to Jamaica was topped with the sweet whipped cream of contracting ringworm. Where? Right on my face. Talk about walking in humility. I went from wanting everyone to recognize my face, to not wanting anyone to see my face.

> Do nothing from selfish ambition or conceit, but in humility count others more significant than yourselves. Let each of you look not only to his own interests, but also to the interests of others. Have this mind among yourselves, which is yours in Christ Jesus, who, though He was in the form of God, did not count equality with

God a thing to be grasped, but emptied Himself, by taking the form of a servant, being born in the likeness of men. And being found in human form, He humbled Himself by becoming obedient to the point of death, even death on a cross. Therefore God has highly exalted Him and bestowed on Him the name that is above every name, so that at the name of Jesus every knee should bow, in heaven and on earth and under the earth, and every tongue confess that Jesus Christ is Lord, to the glory of God the Father.

Philippians 2:3-11

Jesus was humble.

I want to begin this book with this trait because it is not casually associated with being a man. Honestly, our culture tends to think of the opposite as a masculine feature. We understand men to be arrogant, proud, and cocky.

But Jesus wasn't any of that. Jesus was incredibly humble. Jesus had more of a right than anyone to be arrogant. Jesus is God! Romans 11:36 says that "from Him and through Him and to Him are all things." Jesus is not just the manliest man of all time, but He is literally "The Man." If anyone would have had the right to walk around on this earth demanding respect and honor, it would clearly be the very One who created it.

Yet, Jesus never did that. Instead, He chose to become a man and be limited by every human limitation we have to deal with.[1] He elected to be born to a working-class family and be laid in a feeding trough. He decided to leave Heaven, where He was adored and worshiped day in and day out, to enter a world where He was hated, beaten, mistreated, dishonored, and eventually killed.

Why would an all-powerful God choose to do that? Jesus wanted to model for us what it looks like to live for someone other than ourselves. Jesus wanted to show us how to make ourselves less so God would be glorified in our lowliness and others would benefit from our service. After all, if the guy who created all of Heaven and Earth can humble Himself to serve me, what justification do I have to abstain from humility and service to others? I have no right.

Jesus says in Luke 10:27, "Love the Lord your God with all your heart and with all your soul and with all your strength and with all your mind; and, love your neighbor as yourself." In order to love my neighbor

---

1 – Check out Hebrews 2:17 and John 5:19. Even though Jesus was and is God-in-the-flesh, He chose to take on human limitations and show us what it can look like when a human being lives free from sin and in a healthy relationship with the Father.

as myself, I need to first love myself well. Loving who God has made you to be is not arrogance; it's assurance.

In John 13, we see a great picture of Jesus' humility in action. Jesus was at a party with His disciples. He left the room and came back wearing nothing but His undergarments and a towel. Jesus walked to Peter and knelt at his feet. He took off Peter's shoes. After correcting Peter's initial objection, Jesus washed his feet. In fact, Jesus told Peter that if he didn't let Him serve him, then Peter had no relationship with Him.

What type of leader would do this? Jesus is the perfect example of what it looks like to lead by example. Again, we have the King of the Universe serving small, dirty, sinful people. Jesus didn't think of Himself as a slave. He knew He was King. He knew that at anytime, He could order Peter to wash His feet. But, His awareness of His identity as a King didn't keep Him from living like a servant.

Jesus, even though He was King, lived like a servant so that we, even though we are servants, can live as kings.

You want to be a man? **Be humble.**

"The price of success is hard work, dedication to the job at hand, and the determination that whether we win or lose, we have applied the best of ourselves to the task at hand."
~ Vince Lombardi ~

I was lazy in high school. I never did any work that I didn't need to do. By that I mean I calculated my grades and would only finish an assignment in order to keep my grade above a C. If the assignment wouldn't drop my grade below that magic letter, I wouldn't do that assignment.

That's right—this teacher, author, and pastor was a terribly lazy high school student.

I remember the final push to get my grades up. Senior year was here, and I was entering it with a dim 2.5 GPA. I learned that if I earned straight A's, I would be able to raise my GPA to a 3.5, which would earn me the title "Honor Grad."

I wanted that.

Luckily, I was able to take simple electives and a few easy, breezy core classes. I aced them all except one! I sat in the senior awards night expecting to hear my name called. I began to grow anxious, as the alphabetically organized list grew closer.

K…L…M…N…

I waited to hear my last name broadcast through the muffled podium microphone. I was sure I would be standing on the stage with every other honor grad in just a few moments.

…O…P…

After all the names of the honor grads had been called, the crowd applauded. I sat in the front section of the auditorium along with no more than 5 other slackers. I've never felt an embarrassment so slicing. I never thought of myself as the smart kid. This only affirmed that belief more. It's not that I wasn't smart—I was. The problem was my lack of work ethic.

I learned the next day that my graduating GPA was 3.49. True story. I was .01 away from being an Honor Grad, forever proving I was intelligent to my classmates, my teachers, my family, and myself.

That .01 was .01 more time studying, .01 more focus on a test, .01 more pages of homework.

I would work hard at ministry stuff. I would spend my time volunteering, going to church services, praying and evangelizing with my friends. I didn't work hard at my schoolwork because I didn't see it as something meaningful.

That's not what Jesus thinks.

First Thessalonians 4:11 says, "Make it your goal to live a quiet life, minding your own business and working with your hands, just as we instructed you before." Why would The Bible insist that we work hard and humbly? Because God intends for us to look like Him. We were created to be "in His image."

Jesus worked hard and humbly. Until He stepped into ministry, Jesus lived a quiet life. He minded His own business, and He worked with His hands. I love how the King of the Universe chose to live a virtually unknown life, working with His earthly father as a carpenter until He was about 30 years old.

Jesus had a great work ethic. He worked hard. Jesus probably could have spoken any structure or tool into existence (after all, He could have commanded rocks to turn into bread), but He instead chose to build things. Rather than simply speaking a barn or a table into being, Jesus got down and dirty with the wood He was crafting. He put His heart into His work. Based on the detail we see that He put into creation, I'm sure He painstakingly invested into the details of His wooden masterpieces.

I love to read stories from the Gospels about times where Jesus ate dinner at someone's house. I imagine Him walking up to someone's table, looking it up and down, shaking it, and bending over to see if it was level. Can you picture it? I come from a family of builders, and we inspect everything. We knock on the walls to find the studs, and we shift tables to make sure they are level. Can you imagine Jesus asking Mary and Martha who made the table they were about to eat at? Maybe He inquires about how much they paid and determines whether or not the deal was fair or unfair. He probably notices an error or two—errors only a skilled craftsman like Himself would notice. After knocking on the legs and shaking it back and fourth a couple of times, He says, "This is a nice table. Whoever made it did a good job." Maybe He suggests how He would have sculpted the legs to give it a little more style. The disciples are like, "Jesus, sit down. It's fine. The table isn't going to be perfect!"

It's weird to think about Jesus being so normal, but He was. Even though He is fully God, He is also fully man. Jesus likely got cuts and bruises from the wood He crafted. I'm sure He got splinters and scratches too. My friend Steven says, "He probably busted his thumb with the hammer once or twice." [1]

My grandpa Stan was a builder. I remember growing up on building sites—working on a house, a roof, or an extension. I remember the hard work my grandpa put into what he was building. It always had to be perfect. There's an old saying, "Measure twice, cut once." Well, for my grandpa it was more like, "Measure five times, cut once." I never entirely understood his obsession with perfection. Then I realized that he simply wanted to do well. He knew there was a sense of accomplishment that came with a hard day's work. Sitting down at the end of the day—smelling like sweat, sawdust, and Icy Hot—was the

1 – Steven is one of the most loving men of God I know. Many of my greatest ministry memories are with him.

mark of a good work ethic.

I think Jesus smelled like that too.[2] He probably had sawdust in His beard and sweat on his shirt. Like Jesus, my grandpa understood that working hard mattered. He knew that with every measurement, every nail, and every level, he was imparting his heart into his work.

Jesus implores us to work hard at whatever we do because everything matters. To Jesus, there is no division between what is "secular" and what is "sacred."

Here's what I mean by that: We tend to think of what we do in terms of secular or sacred. If I am a businessman, I work in the secular realm. If I am pastor, I work in the sacred realm. We believe that people who work in the sacred realm honor God more with their occupation than those in the secular realm.

That's not the case. Jesus wasn't in "vocational ministry," meaning ministry wasn't His profession. Jesus was a carpenter just like His earthly dad, Joseph. Jesus didn't separate the secular from the sacred. He fused them both together.

---

2 – Probably minus the Icy Hot.

Colossians 3:23 says, "Whatever you do, work at it with all your heart, as working for the Lord, not for human masters." So, whether you are mowing a neighbor's lawn or helping with your church's kids' ministry, work hard and do it well—just like Jesus would.

You want to be a man? **Work hard.**

COURAGE
3

"I learned that courage was not the
absence of fear, but the triumph over it.
The brave man is not he who does not feel afraid,
but he who conquers that fear."
~ Nelson Mandella ~

Courage is a trait that is definitely associated in our culture with being masculine. Have you ever seen Mel Gibson's movie, *The Patriot*? It is the story of a father who stepped into the horrors of the Revolutionary War to fight for his country and family.

29

These stories inspire us.

God has put the desire to be courageous inside of every man. That's why when we watch these heroic movies, we get amped up and ready to fight. We have been created to be men of courage.

Being a man of courage doesn't necessarily mean that you need to stand on the front lines of battle waving Old Glory to rally the troops. But it does mean that in the face of fear and resistance, you keep moving toward where God calls you.

Sometimes God may call you to go somewhere uncomfortable.

Be courageous.

Sometimes God may call you to do something intimidating.

Be courageous.

If, like me, you go to a college at a small university in the middle of rural Michigan, you will have a short list of things to do outside of school. One of the things my friends and I would do was make late night trips to Walmart.

Something special happens after midnight in

Walmart. I don't quite know how to explain it, but it is odd. After midnight, Walmart becomes something that resembles a carnival. Shirts and shoes are optional, and mullets are back in style.

I will never forget what happened one night during this ritual midnight escapade to Walmart. Only two or three checkout lanes were open that night for the line of nearly fifty motley customers waiting to check out. I was among those waiting. My friends and I enjoyed each other's company as we slowly advanced in line.

Then something began to happen in my spirit. I gazed at the long line of people I was standing in. My heart began to hurt for them. In one moment, the weird "Walmart people" simply became *people*. They became moms, dads, sons, daughters—people with a story, people God loves. I was quickly swept up in a feeling of compassion and love.

I heard God speak to me. He said, "Stand on the checkout and preach."

What? No way. That's not God.

I quickly began to discredit what I was hearing in my spirit. The still, small, voice quickly became a swarm of butterflies in my stomach.

I couldn't get the thought out of my head. I knew I

had to be obedient while, at the same time, I couldn't find the courage to stand up in front of this long line of people and randomly preach.

I was scared and nervous and excited all at the same time. My friend Kyle looked at me and asked how I was doing. He noticed how physically distraught I had become.

The next thing I knew, I was standing on the conveyor belt asking for everyone's attention. The line, which had now doubled in the number of shoppers, went silent. Almost immediately after I stood up and spoke, an employee yelled at me, "Boy, get down from there!" I immediately obeyed. I hopped off of the checkout and started preaching the Gospel.

I wrapped the short sermon up with an invitation for prayer. "I'll wait here. If you need prayer, or if you want to give your life to Jesus, come find me." I waited as person after person passed me and exited the store.

Some of the people cussed me out and made fun of me.

Some of them smiled with calm gratitude.

Others simply passed me by while avoiding eye

contact.

Only one man stayed to ask for prayer. With such a small response to the message, I was a bit discouraged. I wrote it off as a test of obedience.

I grew in boldness that day. I gained a confidence that I would have never attained by another experience. Every evangelistic endeavor after that was a cakewalk.

A year later, I was sitting in the cafeteria. Two underclassmen walked up to me and said, "You're the Walmart guy." It had been a year since then; I honestly had no idea what they were talking about. Then they explained how they were struggling with talking to others about Jesus. They had gone to Walmart that night and were waiting in line as I stood on the checkout and preached the Gospel. They shared about how the courage was contagious. They were encouraged to share the Gospel with their friends because I had obeyed the voice of God.

A year after the fact, I learned the reason God asked me to do what I did that night in Walmart. I learned that it was not only to help me gain courage but also to encourage other believers to be courageous with their faith. I'm so glad I obeyed!

Notice what Paul said in the Amplified Bible:

> Be on guard; stand firm in your faith [in God, respecting His precepts and keeping your doctrine sound]. Act like [mature] men and be courageous; be strong.
>
> *1 Corinthians 16:13, AMP*

Other translations say, "Act like men," or, "Be men of courage."

Being courageous is, simply put, facing adversity head-on. A firefighter, when facing a blazing inferno, would most likely attest to feeling a sense of fear for his life. This fear doesn't make him a coward. In fact, it is the fear that makes him courageous. If it weren't for a justifiable fear of death by fire, there would be no courage needed to face it. The firefighter is courageous because he faces the fire despite his fear. And he does not face the fire without reason. He faces the flames to accomplish a mission he has committed to finish.

If what we face is not risky, uncomfortable, unsafe, or worthy of fearing, we do not exercise courage when facing it. Therefore, fear does not deny us our courage; instead, it supplies it.

Jesus was a wonderful example of how to live courageously. Notice His demeanor in Matthew 26 as He cries out to His Father and makes His fears known:

> And going a little farther He fell on His face and prayed, saying, "My Father, if it be possible, let this cup pass from Me; nevertheless, not as I will, but as You will."
>
> *Matthew 26:39*

Jesus was in agony over the torture that was to come. He knew that in just a few minutes, Judas would betray Him. He knew that the Roman guards would beat Him relentlessly. He knew they would twist a crown made of thorns deep into His head. He knew they would nail Him by His hands and feet to a splintery, wooden cross and leave Him for dead as He suffocated and bled. He knew He was going to take on the sins of the entire world—past, present, and future.

In the Garden of Gethsemane, Jesus foresaw the coming events and, even so, faced them with courage.

Did they keep Him from the mission to save the world from death?

No.

Did they cause Him to forsake us?

No.

Jesus had the courage and tenacity to go forward, into the most brutal beating any human would ever endure.

With future pain and death looking Him straight in the eyes, He uttered the most courageous words any man has ever said: "Nevertheless, not as I will, but as You will."

Courageous men do not allow situations to determine their next move. Courageous men focus on God instead of the issue. Jesus saw the goal that God had laid at the end of the path, and He went after it. Courageous men stay focused and steady on God's promises. Courageous men hold on to the hope they have in God's faithfulness, just like the writer of Hebrews instructs us to do:

> Let us hold fast the confession of our hope without wavering, for he who promised is faithful.
>
> *Hebrews 10:23*

You want to be a man? **Be courageous.**

WISDOM
4

"Wisdom is the right use of knowledge. To know is not to be wise. Many men know a great deal, and are all the greater fools for it. There is no fool so great a fool as a knowing fool. But to know how to use knowledge is to have wisdom."
~ Charles Spurgeon ~

I have made many mistakes. I have been very foolish at times. Sometimes I would ask myself, "Is this wise?" and go ahead and do the foolish thing anyway.

The trouble is that we sometimes only think that "wisdom" is nothing more than the restraint demonstrated by older people who lack our creativity or resolve. In reality, wisdom is something much better. Consider what the Bible says:

> For the Lord gives wisdom; from His mouth come knowledge and understanding.
>
> *Proverbs 2:6*

> If any of you lacks wisdom, you should ask God, who gives generously to all without finding fault, and it will be given to you.
>
> *James 1:5*

> When pride comes, then comes disgrace, but with humility comes wisdom.
>
> *Proverbs 11:2*

> The wise in heart accept commands, but a chattering fool comes to ruin.
>
> *Proverbs 10:8*

> Be very careful, then, how you live—not as unwise but as wise, making the most of every opportunity, because the days are evil.
>
> *Ephesians 5:15-16*

After reading these few verses, what does wisdom mean to you? Go ahead... think about it.

When I was in high school, there was this thing called "Planking." It was essentially where you lay face down somewhere and take a picture.[1] You'd then send that picture to your friends or post it on Facebook.

I began my exploits in Planking when my youth pastor, Pastor Tom, started the trend within our youth group. Before I knew it, I had progressed from planking on a table or the floor to planking on a basketball hoop and even a living horse. True story.

At the same time this trend was happening, I was playing a game with Pastor Tom called "Aztec." (I know... I know... we had a lot of trends to keep up with.) Aztec was a game where when we saw a Pontiac Aztec, we would shout, "AZTEC!" and receive a point. These points were worth a great deal of pride and bragging rights. If there was no witness to the Aztec-sighting, the player was required to take a picture of the car, which scientifically documented that an Aztec was, in fact, spotted.

In high school I was a little bit competitive. I figured I could kill two birds with one stone. The thought that

---

1 – Don't judge. I'm sure your generation has something equally ridiculous.

entered my mind was a brilliantly foolish idea. I would plank on a moving Aztec!

Oh yes.

I would lay on top of an Aztec as it drove down the street! I would be legendary. I would be canonized as the greatest Planker/Aztec player in history.

But the question buzzed inside of me: *IS IT WISE?*

The answer was obvious. "No."

I debated with myself but couldn't escape the conclusion. I looked myself in the face (metaphorically speaking) and said, "Casey, you will die." Legendary or not, I made the decision to put on the brakes and listen to the warning in my gut.

In 2 Chronicles, King Solomon was essentially face to face with God. God asked him what he desired. Solomon answered by saying he needed wisdom and understanding.

King Solomon felt insecure about his role as king over Israel, so God gave Solomon wisdom to rightly govern the nation.

This story is incredible. First and foremost, God asked King Solomon what he wanted. Often times we go into prayer frantically telling God what we need as if He doesn't want to give us anything. That's not the case. God wants to give us good gifts because He is a good Father.

When I am praying about healing for someone, I expect that God wants to release that healing. When I am praying for grace to overcome a difficult situation, I believe that God will give it to me. This attitude in prayer is important to grasp as you move forward in your walk with Jesus.

Say this: "God wants to give me good gifts." (We will address this more in Chapter 6.)

Solomon didn't ask for money. He didn't ask for more land or a bigger home. He didn't ask for good weather or good fortune. He asked for wisdom.

Solomon realized the task that was facing him. He knew that his destiny was to rule over the people of Israel—God's chosen people. The responsibility he carried must have been overwhelming.

Have you seen the "before and after" pictures of United States presidents when they first enter office compared to when they leave? When they enter their first term, they are smiling and look healthy and young. When they leave, their hair is gray, their skin is wrinkled, and their eyes are baggy. They don't look as fresh as when they were first sworn into office.

The pressure of leadership is heavy. King Solomon knew this pressure more than anyone, so he asked for what he truly needed: wisdom.

Back to Jesus. If Jesus is fully God, shouldn't He have all wisdom since all wisdom comes from God?

Remember, Jesus was fully human as well.

Everything Jesus did on earth was done within the parameters of human limitation. Jesus modeled the lives we could live once we have been born again by the Holy Spirit.

Jesus needed to grow in wisdom just like we do. Luke 2:52 says, "And Jesus grew in wisdom and stature, and in favor with God and man." Jesus had to grow up too.

Wisdom comes through a connection with The Father. Jesus modeled this truth as well.

> After He had dismissed them, He went up on a mountainside by Himself to pray. Later that night, He was there alone...
>
> *Matthew 14:23*

Jesus went to be alone with the Father regularly. Jesus' time with God was what helped Him grow in wisdom. Jesus connected with the Father and allowed God to direct His steps.

Even at a young age, Jesus was intentional about growing into the man He was destined to be. That's wisdom. Jesus didn't waste His youth. He developed Himself. Before we end this chapter, I want to stress a simple point.

In Luke 2 we read a story about Jesus who, at twelve years old, was interacting with the teachers in the synagogue. Jesus was wise beyond His years because of the time spent with the Father.

Being young isn't an excuse to be foolish.

Boom.

Imma say it again: Being young isn't an excuse to be foolish.[2]

Don't waste your youth.

Why wait to become wise? Why wait to take your

---

2 – Tweet that. Right now, stop what you're doing and tweet that.

@caseynoce "Being young isn't an excuse to be foolish." #Truth #JesusHadABeardBook

* Follow me on Twitter and Instagram @caseynoce

faith seriously?

Why wait?

Those questions are for you to answer, but I'll tell you one great reason not to wait: The enemy is not waiting. 1 Peter 5:8 says, "Your adversary the devil prowls around like a roaring lion, seeking someone to devour." Every second we spend playing games with our faith is another second the enemy has to work unopposed.

How about the people who have never heard of Jesus? Romans 10:14 says, "How then will they call on him in whom they have not believed? And how are they to believe in him of whom they have never heard? And how are they to hear without someone preaching?" People are waiting for the very Gospel we carry! We must be good stewards of that message.

Don't waste your youth on foolishness and playing games with your faith. Step up and be intentional about growing into a man of God. Just like Jesus, set yourself apart from the world by demonstrating the wisdom you have gained through your encounters with God during prayer, worship, scripture study, and sound teaching.

You want to be a man? **Be wise.**

"Nothing is so strong as gentleness,
nothing so gentle as real strength."
~ Francis de Sales ~

When you think about gentleness, what comes to mind? You may think of things like a little pink flower softly dancing in the breeze or a mother rocking her newborn child. You probably aren't thinking of an MMA fighter.

We rarely think masculinity when we think of

gentleness. However, within this chapter, I intend to challenge your definition of the word "gentleness" and present it as something manly and macho.

Oh yes. "Gentleness" may be one of the manliest words around.

We're more likely to associate manliness with the idea of a strong man lifting weights than that of a man who is gentle and meek. So to better understand the concept of gentleness, we will use the mental image of an Olympic weight lifter.

Picture this for a moment: You are at the Olympics, watching the finals of the men's "clean and jerk." In this lift, an athlete will raise the barbell over his head and hold it high above his body until he is completely stable. We watch amazed at the power he harnesses in order to hold on to the weights. His control over the weight is insane! He then escapes from his stance and drops the weight. The crowd goes wild!

Now, we weren't cheering because he dropped the heavy weights. We were cheering because of the control he had over the weight while he was holding it above his head. If the athlete doesn't gain control of the weight, he fails the lift.

Gentleness is the same. It takes a strong man to exhibit the intense control of gentleness rather than outbursts of anger, violence, or frustration. It is easy to react poorly but difficult to react with gentleness.

High school guys are not notorious for being gentle. In fact, the opposite is true. I was the same. I was violent and prone to freaking out.

I played tennis. That's a gentle sport right?

Well, yes, but...

I was not gentle.

You can see the issue there. I spent my time on the court of this etiquette sport doing two things: (1) playing tennis and (2) getting myself into fights.

If you've heard of John McEnroe, that was me. I would launch balls into the parking lot, yell at my opponent for bad calls, and even punch the fence and cut up my knuckles. Looking back at my behavior, I am embarrassed. I am so glad I had parents and a great youth leader named Jim who eventually helped me grow out of that immaturity.

I was not gentle.

Then we found Ducky. That's right—we named our adopted pet duck "Ducky." [1]

---

1 – So creative, right?

Yeah.

We found Ducky at our cottage while he was in the middle of a predicament. And by "predicament," I mean a dog's mouth.

We rescued the little duckling and nursed him back to health.

Holding this little duckling, I had to dig deep and harness the power of gentleness inside of me. Otherwise I would squish this little guy in my mighty man-hands.

The gentleness was always in me. I just needed to focus on using it. I was able to learn how to utilize my gentleness on the tennis court too. As the season progressed, I became better at controlling myself and responding to adversity with a gentle sportsmanship.

If God's Spirit dwells in you, then gentleness is in you.[2] You just need to find it and bring it out.

Imagine with me again…

A young son runs up to his dad, excited and eager to show him his new art project. "Daddy! Daddy! Come

---

2 – Check out Galatians 5:22-23 to see the things the Holy Spirit naturally produces in the lives of those who let Him.

outside! I made something for you!"

The father follows his son outside to the driveway.

With a smile bigger than his face, the boy presents his art project to his father.

The father grits his teeth and holds back his frustration as he sees the so-called "art"…

…engraved deeply in the car door.

Scratched into the smooth, metallic paint are the words, "I Love Dad."

This is a beautiful message, yes – but a terrible medium for this particular masterpiece.

I don't know what your experiences lead you to expect as the dad's response. He could easily overpower the little boy and assert himself, using his physical strength to scold and correct the child. However, a good father doesn't respond with an outburst of anger. A good father is gentle and allows his love to motivate the young son to act rightly.

The father begrudgingly says, "Thanks, kiddo. It's beautiful. But—and I should've set this boundary earlier—we do not scratch messages or artwork into cars."

In reality, a dad's response to something like this may not sound as eloquent as I have written it and may include a few grumbles of frustration, but the message is the same. Responding gently instead of reacting out of frustration or anger shows your internal strength.

Consider the gentle restraint Jesus demonstrated in Luke 22:47-53.

Jesus was in the garden with His disciples. He knew it was time to give up His life, and He was preparing spiritually and emotionally for the moments to come.

After silently praying alone, Jesus heard a rustle in the trees. Turning, He saw the glow of lanterns growing stronger. The mumbling of the guards grew louder and more understandable.

"Where is He, Judas? You said He'd be here."

Then, through a clearing, Jesus made eye contact with Judas. Judas shamefully yet defiantly walked closer and gave Jesus a kiss.

Imagine you're there as a witness to the event.

Everyone is silent. Time has stopped.
The guards gather around Jesus as the tension rises.

But Jesus isn't going anywhere without a fight. Not

tonight.

He throat-chops Judas and roundhouse kicks a guard in the face. He does a back flip and RKO's another—then another.

Peter draws his sword and cuts off someone's ear!

After executing a series of ninja-like moves, and with all the guards lying on the ground motionless, Jesus waves His hand in front of his face (John Cena-Style) while standing over Judas' limp body and says, "You can't see Me."

Hold on.

Wait, nope...

That's not what happened.

Actually, the only thing that was true about that story was Peter reacting violently by cutting off a guard's ear.[3]

Here's the real version—you know, out of the Bible:

---

3 – By the way, Peter wasn't aiming for his ear. Peter was trying to kill this guy! Nobody tries to cut off another dude's ear. But people do try to cut off other dude's heads.

While he was still speaking, there came a crowd, and the man called Judas, one of the twelve, was leading them. He drew near to Jesus to kiss Him, but Jesus said to him, "Judas, would you betray the Son of Man with a kiss?" And when those who were around Him saw what would follow, they said, "Lord, shall we strike with the sword?" And one of them struck the servant of the high priest and cut off his right ear. But Jesus said, "No more of this!" And He touched his ear and healed him. Then Jesus said to the chief priests and officers of the temple and elders, who had come out against him, "Have you come out as against a robber, with swords and clubs? When I was with you day after day in the temple, you did not lay hands on me. But this is your hour, and the power of darkness. Then they seized him and led him away, bringing him into the high priest's house, and Peter was following at a distance.

Luke 22:47-53

Check out what Jesus did. He corrected Peter, and then He picked up the man's bloody ear and stuck it back on his head.

The guy (named Malchus) was miraculously healed. A

man who is there to arrest Jesus and take Him to be executed is in this moment healed by the gentle Man, Jesus.

Imagine Malchus walking into town after turning Jesus in. People are stopping him, saying, "Malchus, why is there blood all over your tunic?"

"Well," Malchus replies, "Peter, one of Jesus' disciples, cut off my ear."

"Really? But you still have both ears."

"Yeah…" Malchus replies, "Jesus—He, He touched it… and… it's fine now. I don't know how to explain it, but… He healed me."

Jesus did not respond to His arrest with anger, violence, or a display of physical force. Even though at any time He could have called armies of angels to rescue Him, instead Jesus told the guards that they wouldn't need their weapons.

Jesus essentially said in verses 52 and 53, "You can put away your weapons. I'm not going to fight. Why would I start being violent now?"

Even in an incredibly tense moment, Jesus reacted with gentleness and willingly gave Himself up. I can't imagine a more justifiable time to react without gentleness. Yet Jesus set the bar higher once more, this time through gentleness.

You want to be a man? **Be Gentle.**

"Faith is a living, daring confidence in God's grace, so sure and certain that a man could stake his life on it a thousand times."
~ **Martin Luther** ~

Confidence is tricky. We want people to be confident, but not *too* confident. A balance of confidence and humility is critical. Jesus modeled that balance wonderfully.

Without being tethered together with humility,

confidence quickly becomes pride. Jesus had all the confidence in the world, yet none of the pride.

As a teenager, I attended a worship event called "Ignite." The guy who was preaching was really spilling out his heart in a great message. Needless to say, God was moving.

Suddenly, God spoke something to my heart about the preacher. I felt like He wanted me to share it with the preacher.

I knew it was God.

I started getting butterflies in my stomach as I thought about approaching him and sharing the message God had put on my heart. I couldn't seem to muster the confidence. I found every excuse not to talk to him.

He's busy.

I don't want to interrupt.

I've got to be getting home.

He's probably tired.

I'm just a 10th grader.

He wouldn't listen to me anyway…

I left and started driving home. While in the car, I felt the Holy Spirit stir me even more. I received a boost of confidence and drove back to the church.

I walked in the lobby and timidly told the preacher the message God had given me. He received the message and asked me for prayer. In that moment, I wasn't a scrawny 10th grader anymore; I was a prophet of God!

The enemy was feeding me lies about myself to try and keep me from relaying God's words. The message was not from me but from God, yet I allowed my own insecurities and the lies that I had believed to dictate my behavior. I almost completely chickened out because I wasn't thinking about the role God had given me as His spokesman.

The Holy Spirit gave me a spiritual confidence that day, and it has only grown stronger since.

Even if I don't have a strong confidence in myself, I can have a strong confidence in God's word and in my relationship with Him. In Jeremiah 9:24, God says, "…but let him who boasts boast in this, that he understands and knows Me, that I am the Lord who practices steadfast love, justice, and righteousness in the earth…"

Hebrews 4:16 says, "Let us then approach God's throne of grace with confidence[1] so that we may receive mercy and find grace to help us in our time of need." Can you imagine living with a confidence so great that you can walk up to God in Heaven and address Him face to face? This is the type of confidence we should live with.

Have you heard of Esther? She was the queen of Persia. You can read about her in the Bible in the aptly-named book of Esther. She was a Jew, yet because of her beauty, she was chosen to be the Persian queen and marry King Xerxes.

To make a long story short, Xerxes was advised to annihilate every Jew in Persia. He was ready to follow through with his plan, but this would mean killing his wife! (Although, at the time, Xerxes didn't know that Esther was a Jew.)

Esther learned of the plot to wipe out the Jews and knew she had to step in to save her people. In this time period, if someone were to enter the courts of the king without an invitation, two things could happen. Either the king would have the intruder killed on the spot, or he would extend his scepter to them and welcome them in.

---

1 – Many translations say "boldness."

Esther knew what she had to do. She barged into the king's courts uninvited.

I love to imagine the tense nature of the moment. I can hear the sound of the doors bursting open as Esther enters and the echo of the doors slamming against the walls of the throne room. The guards take a step toward her to arrest her, waiting for the king's order.

Xerxes pauses, everyone in the room waits for the order. Will he have his queen executed in front of him or will he pardon her?

They watch him raise his scepter to her.

Talk about confidence! Esther was confident in who she was as the beloved of the king. She entered his courts prepared to save her people with confidence.

This confidence only comes through knowledge of one's identity. Esther knew the king loved her and that she had favor in his sight. The same is true for all of us. God loves us, and He wants to pour out His favor on us.

Often times we approach God in prayer without really expecting to receive what we ask for. We pray, "God, if You could…I mean, if You want to—it's not really a big deal—but would You maybe help me with…"

What type of prayer is that?

We can confidently approach God and ask Him for what we need. He wants to love us.

My friend, Art gives great insight to this subject in his book *Limitless Hope:*

> When I'm out to eat with my wife, I might say, "Hey Honey, could you please pass the salt?" Then my wife will naturally respond in her best evil villain voice, "You fool! Can't you see that I'm enjoying my food? How dare you interrupt me to give you salt! It isn't my will!"
>
> Of course, you know that isn't true! Passing the salt is a piece of cake for my wife. She gladly puts down her fork and passes the shaker. In this case, Robin's will was simply to love me. If her will was specifically to pass me the salt, then she would have passed it without my asking. But if she willed to love me, then my asking was the sole reason for the salt being passed. Whether she wanted to pass it or not is irrelevant—her love for me responded with action when the salt was

requested. The salt wasn't the point. She "willed" to love me.[2]

Art is able to confidently ask his wife, Robin, for the salt because he has confidence in her love for him. In the same way, we can boldly ask God for what we need when we have a confidence in His love for us.

And God has everything that we need! Whenever we pray and ask God for what we need, we demonstrate that we believe and are confident that He is able to answer our prayers

It wouldn't make much sense to ask your dad if you could borrow his car if your dad didn't have a car. You would never ask him for something He doesn't have. So the very act of asking is evidence that we believe our Father can provide.

Confident prayers come not only from a confidence in God but a confidence in who you are.

Read the following verses.

Pray about them.

---

2 – Art Thomas, *Limitless Hope*, Supernatural Truth Productions, LLC. Page 129. I'd also recommend you check out his other books, *The Word of Knowledge in Action* and *Spiritual Tweezers*.

Remember them when you pray:

- Q **You are a child of God.** – *John 1:12*
- Q **You are chosen**. – *Ephesians 1:5*
- Q **You are free.** – *Romans 6:6*
- Q **God knows you.** – *Jeremiah 1:5*
- Q **You are a new creation.** – *2 Corinthians 5:17*
- Q **You are part of the Body of Christ.**
  – *1 Corinthians 12:27*
- Q **You are the Temple of the Holy Spirit.**
  – *1 Corinthians 6:19*
- Q **You are alive in Christ and seated in Heavenly places.** – *Colossians 3:1* and *Ephesians 2:6*

Matthew 4:23 says, "Jesus went throughout Galilee, teaching in their synagogues, preaching the gospel of the kingdom, and healing every disease and sickness among the people." Jesus walked around town with a confidence in who He was. Jesus knew He had a relationship with the Father. He boldly proclaimed in John 10:30, "I and the Father are One." He knew that He could heal the sick because He knew the Father's desire was to heal the sick.[3]

Jesus knew He could preach with authority because

---

3 – Jesus perfectly represented the Father (Hebrews 1:3, John 14:9) and only did the Father's will (John 6:38), and Jesus healed everyone who came to Him for it (Matthew 4:24; 8:16; 9:35; 12:15; 14:35-36; Mark 6:56; Luke 4:40; 6:18-19; Acts 10:38).

He knew what the Father was speaking. Jesus knew the Father and acted like it. This confidence manifested itself in everything He did.

Notice the order: Confidence comes from WHO we are and then results in WHAT we do. When we follow this model of confidence, we keep our identity established in God. We can get into trouble when we flip-flop the two. When our confidence comes from WHAT we do and results in WHO we are, we miss out on living a fulfilled life, confidently connected with God.

Identity is the root of confidence; action is the result.

Want to be a man? **Be Confident.**

STRENGTH
7

"Strength does not come from winning.
Your struggles develop your strengths.
When you go through hardships and decide
not to surrender, that is strength."
~ Arnold Schwarzenegger ~

Finally, an attribute we all think of as manly. Have you ever had someone tell you to "man up"? What are they implying? When I hear that phrase, I associate it with being strong or tough. I tell myself to "man up" all the time.

I spent an entire winter in Rome, Italy, doing missions work. Going anywhere alone is tough, especially for me—I am incredibly extroverted. So, this trip was a challenge. I lived by myself and spent most of my time by myself. The few friends that I did have lived 30 minutes away; so after a good days work, I often went home and hung out with Jesus.

After a few weeks of acclimating to the new culture and language, I decided to find a gym—somewhere to spend some free time while getting to know locals and learning the language. So I joined Crossfit.[1]

I didn't really know what I was getting into at the time. But I'm an athlete, so figured I could handle it. The first workout was, well, **HONEST**. Here's what I mean by that: I found out rather quickly that I was incredibly weak and out of shape.

I began to regret the pounds and pounds of pasta, bread, and gelato I'd been eating. I left the gym sweating more than I knew possible (or should I say "pasta-ble"?).

Anyone??

No?

---

1 – What type of Crossfitter would I be without publically bragging about it? Btw, Jesus did Crossfit. Maybe that could be another book.

Sometimes I'm funny.

I'll move on.

The next day I could barely move. My friends will attest to it. The lead pastor at the church I was at referenced my aches and pains as a sermon illustration![2]

I couldn't hide behind my athletic façade anymore; it was time to get fit.

I went back.

I was paired with a super shredded Italian man for the team workout. Even though he was intimidating, he pushed me to work harder—not just because he encouraged me, but also because I didn't want to let him down. I wanted to push him too.

It's important to have a friend who can push you to become better.

I remember the pain of the workout. I remember the sweat and nausea in the midst of the lifting and exercise. I was drained at the end. But when I left the gym, I left with a sense of accomplishment and newly found strength.

---

2 – Thanks for that, Pastor Rick.

I could feel the post-workout "high."

A few weeks later, I was having an off-day. Nothing was really going my way. I went to the gym, as I had made my habit. It was an individual workout, and I wasn't on my game. I cheated the workout. I didn't lift the weight I should have, and I skipped some reps.

I left the gym feeling gross. I felt like I wasted the last hour. I felt weaker.

I didn't have the post-workout high. Instead I felt low.

That night I had a dream where I returned home to Michigan, and I felt like I did after that day's workout. As I walked off the plane in my dream, I began to regret the time I wasted in Rome. I suddenly realized that I hadn't made an impact because I was lazy and disconnected.

In the dream, I started screaming, "I need to go back!" But I couldn't. My journey was over, and I had wasted my time. I hadn't pushed myself. I wasn't strong enough.

I woke up from the dream in a panic. I knew it was from the Lord. I was homesick and tired of the transition. I was tired of struggling to speak the language and fatigued from working so hard.

I knew I had to "man up" and do what I went there to do. I had a mission ahead of me, and I was going to give the next couple months everything I had. Just like the workout, I wanted to arrive home tired and yet stronger.

I am glad to say, I did.

I arrived at the Detroit airport months later with a sense of accomplishment just like the post-workout high. When I saw my friends at baggage claim, my trip was finally finished. I knew I had given the people of Rome everything I had. I knew I had left it all in the gym, so to speak. I knew I was stronger.

Jesus modeled this strength to us. He never quit, even in the face of death.

> Just as there were many who were appalled at Him—His appearance was so disfigured beyond that of any human being and His form marred beyond human likeness…
>
> *Isaiah 52:14, NIV*

When the guards were done with Jesus, you couldn't tell who He was.

That's strong.

Jesus saw the prize at the end of the pain, and He had the strength to endure until that prize was won. That prize is the joy of relationship with you and me.[3]

Jesus was beaten more than anyone! Did you catch that in the verse above? His face was "disfigured beyond that of any human being."

How can this be? Romans 6:23 says that the payment for sin is death. Well, Jesus never sinned, which means that the only way that He was going to die was if He willfully gave up His own life.

How do we know Jesus took the greatest beating of all? Anyone else would have died earlier in the process because anyone else would have sinned during their life.

Jesus, however, was sinless. Jesus couldn't have had His life taken from Him; He needed to give it.

Jesus endured more than the death penalty for you and me.

Listen to what the psalmist prophesied the Messiah—

---

3 – Check out Hebrews 12:2

Jesus—would endure at His execution:

> "I am poured out like water,
>   and all my bones are out of joint;
> my heart is like wax;
>   it is melted within my breast;
> my strength is dried up like a potsherd,
>   and my tongue sticks to my jaws;
>   you lay me in the dust of death.
> For dogs encompass me;
>   a company of evildoers encircles me;
> they have pierced my hands and feet – I
> can count all my bones—
>   they stare and gloat over me;
> they divide my garments among them,
>   and for my clothing they cast lots.
> But you, O Lord, do not be far off!
>   O you my help, come quickly to my
> aid!"

Psalm 22:14-19

Talk about strength. He could count all of His bones?! His bones were all out of joint?! His heart was melting in His chest?! His hands and feet were pierced?!

The descriptions of the torture Jesus endured are disturbing. Even the guards who crucified Him noticed His strength. (See Matthew 27:54, Mark 15:39, and Luke 23:47.)

Not only did Jesus take the most brutal beating of all time, He also carried His cross and carried our sin. And it wasn't over until Jesus released His spirit into the Father's hands. (See Luke 23.)

Jesus knew what it meant to "man up." He knew what strength was. He knew that He needed to push through and endure the pain, because it would be worth it!

I don't know the challenges you face, but I do know that Jesus understands your pain. Jesus knows the struggle.

Jesus has the strength you need to endure and overcome life's obstacles. Life is a roller-coaster of highs and lows. In that context, Paul says in Philippians 4:13, "I can do all things through Him who strengthens me."

It's not our strength that we rely on; it's Jesus' strength—and He is strong.

Want to be a man? **Be Strong.**

JOY
8

"Man cannot live without joy; therefore when he is deprived of true spiritual joys it is necessary that he become addicted to carnal pleasures."
~ Thomas Aquinas ~

Ken was the principle at the first school I worked at. Ken is one of the most joyful men I know. He is always smiling and singing. He glows with the joy of the Lord.

Every morning, I would come into the school and

walk around with him as he greeted every student and teacher by name. He would walk into a class and begin to sing a song—his "Good Morning, Dear Father" song. It went something like this:

> "Good morning, dear Father,
> I offer to You
> my words, thoughts, and actions
> in all that I do."

Occasionally he'd throw in a few funny lines and playful encouragement. Still the message stayed the same: We should start our day focusing on God.

I learned later on why he sings that song with the kids. It is an overflow of his personal life. Every morning for the past couple decades, Ken wakes up and sings this song to God. The rest of the day, he is joyfully living with God as his focus.

Does Ken mess up? Sure! Are there days when he may be less joyful? Certainly. He's a human just like you or me. But being human is not an excuse to live a dreary and grumpy life.

Jesus was fully human, and He was joyful.

Jesus told jokes. We may not recognize them as funny today, but believe me, 2,000+ years ago in Israel, these jokes were hilarious. Hebrew humor was very much hyperbole and over-exaggeration. So when Jesus said in Mark 4:21, "Is a lamp brought in to be put under a basket, or under a bed, and not on a stand?" you can expect a big laugh from the crowd. The people who heard that would have been floored!

"Take a lamp… *laughter* …and put it under a basket… *wheezing* …that's not where a lamp goes!"

Sure enough, if a typical Midwestern girl was somehow present in this ancient Middle Eastern culture, she would have said, "LOL…I literally can't even…" as she sipped her pumpkin spice latte.

Jesus was funny. He was a joyful person. Jesus wasn't some stingy, grumpy curmudgeon. Jesus was full of joy.[1]

The number one trait people identify with me is my joy. I've come to accept that. I'm always joyful. I whistle while I work, sing to the radio, and laugh a lot.

Now read carefully. I am always joyful, but I am not always happy. I have learned that happiness is conditional—based on my circumstances—while joy is unconditional—based on my relationship with God.

---

1 – Check out Luke 10:21.

I was sitting in a practice room at Spring Arbor when my mom called to tell me my Grandma Pauline had passed away. When I put down the phone, I sat quietly on the piano bench. I was waiting to feel the grief and depression. It didn't come. Instead, memories and good thoughts about her filled my mind.

I wasn't happy, but I still had my joy. I started playing the piano and singing to Jesus. A song spontaneously emerged from my heart:

> Even when I'm worried,
> Even when I'm feeling blue,
> Even when I don't know what to do,
> I will trust in You.

I sang this simple chorus over and over again. My heart was secure. I could feel the presence of God fill the room and comfort me. His comfort fortified my joy.

The joy I felt in that moment was far from conditional. It wasn't based on my circumstances. The joy I felt was based on God's faithfulness.

Even in our lowest moments, God is with us. Even in the tough times we can have joy.

Remember the beating we talked about in the last

chapter? Read what the writer of Hebrews says about that:

> Therefore, since we are surrounded by so great a cloud of witnesses, let us also lay aside every weight, and sin which clings so closely, and let us run with endurance the race that is set before us, looking to Jesus, the founder and perfecter of our faith, who *for the joy that was set before Him endured the cross*, despising the shame, and is seated at the right hand of the throne of God.
>
> *Hebrews 12:1-2, emphasis added*

Jesus endured the cross for the joy that was set before Him. He knew that the outcome of His sacrifice and suffering would result in gaining you and me.

We are the reward of His suffering. We are His joy. Jesus takes pleasure in us.[2]

Just like a best friend, Jesus is excited to spend time with us and know us more. Jesus endured for the joy of being with us. Psalms 30:5 says, "...weeping may stay for the night, but rejoicing comes in the morning" (NIV).

This supernatural joy is available to us. Even in the

---

2 – Check out Psalm 149:4.

darkest spiritual nights, we can have joy because we know the end result.

> You make known to me the path of life;
> You will fill me with joy in Your presence,
> with eternal pleasures at Your right hand.
> *Psalms 16:11, NIV*

The God who created all of Heaven and Earth loves us and offers us eternal life with Him! According to Jesus in John 17:3, eternal life is knowing the Father and the Son through the Holy Spirit. This has ramifications for today and for eternity.

There is an assurance we have in Jesus that if we accept His free gift of salvation, we will be saved!

What could possibly make you more joyful?

In the midst of pain, we can realize that joy comes in the morning, and "His mercies are new every morning." [3]

I wonder how your day would change with this perspective.

I can tell you from experience, this joy is real! When I

---

3 – Check out Lamentations 3:22-23.

keep my mind focused on God, the only possible outcome is a joyful day.

What does it matter if I have a flat tire?

What does it matter if I was cut off in traffic?

What does it matter if I forgot my coffee?

It really doesn't. We can't let those things steal our joy. Our joy comes from Jesus. Just like Him, we need to live life with the end result in mind.

For the joy set before us, we need to live.

You want to be a man? **Be joyful.**

COMPASSION
9

"As Christians, our compassion is simply
a response to the love that God
has already shown us."
~ **Steven Curtis Chapman** ~

I don't like big cities. They've always stressed me out. I live in a small town, and there isn't much hustle and bustle.

Yet in all of my travels, I have been to and lived in big cities. It wasn't until a trip to Chicago, though, that I realized why I don't really like big cities.

It's compassion.

When I am surrounded by thousands of people, I become overwhelmed with the reality that many of them don't know Jesus. It breaks my heart. I've always prayed that God will give me His heart. I didn't realize that in some measure, He already did.

When I walk through big cities, I am consumed with God's compassion. There are so many people who are lost and broken. Whether they are rich or poor, they need Jesus. I can only imagine the extent to which God's heart hurts for them.

The compassion for these people has driven me to action. Compassion without action will fester into depression. If your compassion doesn't lead you to initiate change, it will lead you to a sad life overwhelmed with the burden of the lost.

Some people fall into the trap of depression because of their mishandled compassion. They walk around and mope about all the wrong things in the world but never fight to make those wrongs right.

When you feel compassion for people, you need to respond with action. God is gifting you with compassion so you can make a difference.

People are hurting, yes; but moping around and complaining about these realities are not going to change anything. We need to get up and do something. Getting up and doing something may not be convenient, but it is necessary.

I was known for many things on the campus of Spring Arbor University. Among the guys on my floor, I was known for my pranks.[1]

I would spend a significant amount of money to decorate my Residence Assistant's dorm room each holiday. Halloween, Christmas, Valentines Day, etc. And this was not just simple decoration. No. This was a spectacle! I crammed more gaudy decorations into that tiny dorm room than Clark Griswold would have.

Ben, my RA, would walk into his room after class and stand awestruck at the beauty of his newly decorated room.

One Valentine's Day I realized that spending that money on Ben really made his day. It felt good to make someone happy. As I went to bed that night, my roommate and I began to brainstorm. We realized the great need in Jackson, the city just next to Spring

---

1 – DISCLAIMER: I will not confess to any pranks I have allegedly committed heretofore. I also discourage pranking in a vandalistic fashion. Pranking is an art that must be carried out in a respectable manner. Prank at your own risk.

Arbor.

There were so many people in Jackson who needed help. We'd see it nearly every day. Homeless men and women would walk the streets looking for change. We met families who were struggling to provide the basic needs for their children.

After encountering the brokenness and weariness of the impoverished, God does something to your heart. He gives you a seed of compassion. It's up to us how we tend to that seed. Either we water it and let it grow or we neglect it and watch it die.

My roommate Zach and I realized that we had to do something to shine at least a little light in this city.

We figured with 2,000 students on campus, even if everyone contributed a quarter, we'd have $500 to give to a family or person in need.

We dreamed up a new non-profit organization.

Within the next few weeks, we were registered as a non-profit in the state of Michigan. It was amazing how fast it grew. We would collect a "love offering" every Sunday night. We'd spread out around the campus and knock on every dorm room door.

Within the first 4 months, we raised over $3,000! We

were able to pay electric bills, fill gas tanks, buy dinners, pay for car repairs, buy gifts for kids, and even pay rent to keep families from falling into homelessness!

We watered and cultivated that small seed of compassion that God had planted in our hearts. It grew into a ministry that spread the love of God to people who desperately needed it.

We called it *Love Ambush*. We would ambush people with the love of God in practical ways. All it took was a little seed of compassion.

Jesus was led by compassion. He lived a practical life of influence.

> And Jesus went throughout all the cities and villages, teaching in their synagogues and proclaiming the gospel of the kingdom and healing every disease and every affliction. When he saw the crowds, he had compassion for them, because they were harassed and helpless, like sheep without a shepherd. Then he said to his disciples, "The harvest is plentiful, but the laborers are few; therefore pray earnestly to the Lord of the harvest to send out laborers into his harvest."
>
> *Matthew 9:35-38*

Jesus was "moved with compassion." He saw the people, felt compassion for them, and went to work. After that, He challenged us to follow in His footsteps because the field is big while the team of workers is small. The world needs more people who are moved by compassion to influence their personal world.

Notice how Jesus went about His busy life while allowing leeway for compassion-led ministry:

> After this there was a feast of the Jews, and Jesus went up to Jerusalem. Now there is in Jerusalem by the Sheep Gate a pool, which is called in Hebrew, Bethesda, having five porches. In these lay a great multitude of sick people, blind, lame, paralyzed, waiting for the moving of the water. For an angel went down at a certain time into the pool and stirred up the water; then whoever stepped in first, after the stirring of the water, was made well of whatever disease he had. Now a certain man was there who had an infirmity thirty-eight years. When Jesus saw him lying there, and knew that he already had been in that condition a long time, He said to him, "Do you want to be made well?"

The sick man answered Him, "Sir, I have no man to put me into the pool when the water is stirred up; but while I am coming, another steps down before me."

Jesus said to him, "Rise, take up your bed and walk." And immediately the man was made well, took up his bed, and walked.

And that day was the Sabbath. The Jews therefore said to him who was cured, "It is the Sabbath; it is not lawful for you to carry your bed."

He answered them, "He who made me well said to me, 'Take up your bed and walk.'"

Then they asked him, "Who is the Man who said to you, 'Take up your bed and walk'?" But the one who was healed did not know who it was, for Jesus had withdrawn, a multitude being in that place. Afterward Jesus found him in the temple, and said to him, "See, you have been made well. Sin no more, lest a worse thing come upon you."

The man departed and told the Jews that it was Jesus who had made him well.

John 5:1-15, NKJV

Jesus was going about His business in Jerusalem when He noticed a man who was paralyzed waiting at the Pool of Bethesda. Jesus responded out of compassion for this man and went to heal him. After Jesus healed the man, He ran away.

There are three things I want to highlight in this story:

◗ **First, Jesus was trying to lay low.** He knew that the Jewish leaders would want to arrest Him. He was still waiting for the proper time to give Himself over to the hands of His accusers. Jesus wasn't going to give up His life until He fulfilled every last remaining prophecy about the Messiah.

◗ **Second, people would bring their loved-ones into the pool after an angel had touched the water.** This man had no one to help him into the pool. Because of this, he had watched people get healed day after day while he sat paralyzed. It's hard to imagine that no one saw this man and thought, *Wow, this poor guy has been here for years and has yet to make it to the water. I ought to help him.* No. There was no compassion for this man. Not even the disciples noticed him! But Jesus did. Jesus knew this man's condition. Jesus knew that he had no one to help him into the pool. Jesus was moved by compassion for the man, and it led to a release of healing for him.

○ **And third, Jesus had to hightail it out of there.** Again, Jesus couldn't cause too much ruckus until it was time. After He healed the man, He ran away. The man who was healed didn't even know who Jesus was. It all happened so fast. Jesus diverted from His original schedule, which was to lay low, so that He could minister to the hopeless man He saw.

Compassion moved Jesus. He was different than everyone else at that pool.

There were many people there. The gates were places where lots of people congregated. Not one of them noticed this hopeless man.

The people who wanted to receive healing didn't notice him.

The family members didn't notice him.

The Pharisees didn't notice him.

The disciples didn't notice him.

But Jesus noticed him.

Who do you notice that no one else notices? Who has God given you compassion for? Is it a person, a people group, a nation?

Whoever it is, God has given you compassion for them so that you can minister to them. A man doesn't back down from this mandate.

You want to be a man? **Be compassionate.**

POWER
10

"No one has, at any time, any right to
expect success unless he first obtains the
outpouring of power from on high."
~ **Charles Finney** ~

What is power? Imagine, for a moment, a
Phillips-head screwdriver. It is a relatively
simple tool—handle at one-end and a plus-
shaped tip on the other. It works. It is useable.
However, if you are building something large and
need to screw in hundreds of screws, a power drill

with a Phillips-head bit will make you a much more efficient builder.

I remember when my uncle and I rebuilt the deck at my grandparents' cottage. I was in high school and was excited to help. The deck was fairly large and required a lot of time removing the old wood.

Let me pause in the story to address a simple truth that I cannot ignore. When God begins a new work in you, the old, rotted stuff has to go. It wouldn't make much sense to build a brand new deck over an old, rotted one.

Chew on that for a bit, and then we can get back to the story…

After we finished the demolition, we were ready to build the new deck. We cut the wood and laid it down on the baseboards. I went around to every stud and drilled a small hole into the decking. I drilled hundreds of holes. Then, after the pre-drilling, I went through and drove the screws into the holes.

This process took a couple Saturdays. I put a lot of work into that deck. My uncle and I worked hard to finish the project and were (and still are) proud of the result of our labor.

I couldn't imagine building that deck without the

power drill. It made the task simple. It made the load light. It made the work efficient. It would have taken ten times the effort, strength, and time to pre-drill every hole and drive every screw into its place with a traditional Phillips-head screwdriver. The power drill was vital to our completion of the task at hand.

That's what the power of the Holy Spirit does in our lives. The work is always there, but the power that God gives us helps to accomplish the work with less toil and more efficiency.

Jesus breathed on His disciples in John 20:22 and said, "Receive the Holy Spirit." After that, Jesus commanded them to "go into all the world and preach the Gospel." (See Matthew 28:18-20.)

Are you following this storyline? First, Jesus released the Holy Spirit to dwell within His disciples, just as He had promised. Second, He revealed His plan to spread His Gospel to the world.

But the story doesn't end there. After Jesus shared what we call the "Great Commission," He said (and I'm paraphrasing), "Not so fast!" [1]

I can imagine the disciples getting a bit jumpy, ready

---

1 – Check out Luke 24:49 and Acts 1:4-8.

to release this Gospel into the world for the first time! The culmination of God's plan for salvation had taken place, and now it was time for all of the earth to know!

Yes! Let's go! Let's tell the world!

Not so fast...

Jesus said to wait for power from heaven, which the Father had promised. (See Luke 24:49.)

Jesus knew that the job ahead would be difficult. It would require some serious power tools. We cannot rely on our own talents and our own strength to fulfill the Great Commission; we need the power of the Holy Spirit.

The Holy Spirit is called the Helper in John 14:26.[2] We need His help to walk in the same power that Jesus walked in. This is why Jesus told the disciples to wait. He wanted them—and us—to be well-equipped to handle the task ahead of us.

The best part is, the disciples did wait! They didn't really understand exactly what they were waiting for. All they knew was that they needed to wait for the

---

2 – See John 14:26. This Greek word means Helper, Comforter, Protector, and Advocate. The Holy Spirit has your back.

power of the Holy Spirit to cover them. They didn't know everything that would entail. That is, until the Day of Pentecost:

> When the day of Pentecost arrived, they were all together in one place. And suddenly there came from heaven a sound like a mighty rushing wind, and it filled the entire house where they were sitting. And divided tongues as of fire appeared to them and rested on each one of them. And they were all filled with the Holy Spirit and began to speak in other tongues as the Spirit gave them utterance.
>
> *Acts 2:1-4*

What happened in that house looked chaotic from the outside. In fact, if you read on, people were mocking them and speculating the meaning of it all.

The house was not just filled with the sound of a rushing wind, or fire, or the Gospel being preached in many languages; the house was filled with the power of the Holy Spirit.

The apostles in that house encountered some wild signs and wonders. It is easy to get caught up in the events that took place that day. But Jesus didn't say to go and live in the house where the power shows up. He said, "Go into all the world."

The mission Jesus gave is a necessary component of the Christian life. After this outpouring of the Holy Spirit, the event that took place on the Day of Pentecost that revealed the purpose of the Spirit's power is this:

> ...and there were added that day about three thousand souls.
>
> *Acts 2:41*

Pentecost isn't about wind, fire, or speaking in other tongues; Pentecost is about power for sharing the Gospel. Pentecost is about souls being saved. Pentecost is about the apostles, you, and me, receiving the power we need to share the life-transforming truth of the Gospel in a lost world.

Just think about Peter—a compulsive fisherman who received the power of the Holy Spirit and preached the Gospel to three thousand men immediately after. He went from denying Jesus in front of three people to preaching Jesus in front of three thousand, plus.

This transformation is possible for every believer!

Place yourself in the story. What happens when you receive the power of the Holy Spirit?

Beyond the physical evidence...

Beyond the emotion…

Beyond the experience…

You will have the power to share the Gospel! Things that used to be difficult will become easy. Receiving this power requires nothing on your part other than looking to the Gift-Giver and opening up your hands.

Are you tired of not having the courage to witness to your friends?

Do you want your prayers to affect people?

Do you want to lay hands on the sick and watch them get well?

Do you want to silence the lies of the enemy?

Do you want to walk in holiness and stand strong against temptation?

Do you want to impact this world with the Gospel of Jesus?

The power of the Holy Spirit is for you. Ask for it, receive it, and walk in it.

Want to be a man? **Be Empowered.**

"Love can break your bones. But broken bones
tell stories, and broken bones sing songs."
~ John Mark McMillan ~

What does love mean to you? The world
defines love in many different ways.

Some ways are lighthearted, like, "I *love* that movie!"

Some are friendly, like, "I *love* him. He's a great guy."

Some are passionate, like, "I *love* Chipotle." [1]

There are different uses of the word "love" in our culture. I don't want to tear them all down and say that our perception of love is completely incorrect, because it's not. However, I would like to define love in a different way.

Simply put, love is selflessness.

Jesus said there is no greater love than for a person to lay down his life for his friends.[2] This self-sacrificial love of friendship is the greatest form of love. Deeper than any love song and stronger than any romantic drama—love that places another above oneself is the deepest love of all.

This is sacrifice.

This is selflessness.

This is real love.

Ultimately, the way love becomes real is through sacrifice. Whether that sacrifice is time, money, energy—it doesn't matter. A sacrifice must be made

---

1 – Why is guac extra??

2 – John 15:13

in order to adequately show love to another.

We watch it in the movies all the time. We hear it in songs. We see it on TV. Love requires a selfless sacrifice.

Have you seen *Star Wars, Episode V: The Empire Strikes Back*? There is a scene where Princess Leia and Han Solo are saying goodbye to each other before Han is frozen in carbonite. Leia stands back to watch as Han slowly descends into the chamber. She says, "I love you."

Han responds with a still tone, "I know."

I love this scene! It shows love. Han didn't need to say it back. They loved each other, and that was clear by the sacrifices each had made for the other, not by cheap talk.

Love requires a selfless sacrifice. I specify that the sacrifice must be selfless because we can all sacrifice selfishly. You do it every time you buy something for yourself. You don't sacrifice your money to the store because you love the store but because you want something from them. Similarly, I can sacrifice something I want for you so that you "owe me one" later.

That isn't the type of love Jesus models. He doesn't

hold anything over our heads and try to make us feel guilty for not doing things for Him in return.

There is and will always be the teaching that "Jesus gave His life for you, so you need to give your life to Him." I do agree with the implications that we should live a life dedicated to Jesus with everything we have and are. However, Jesus didn't love us first in order to obligate us to love Him back. He loved us first so that we could be free to choose to love Him back.

> We love because He first loved us.
> *1 John 4:19*

The reason we live our life of sacrifice for Him is not because of some obligation to pay Jesus back. The reason we live for Jesus is because He is so worth living for! There is no greater life outside of knowing Jesus.

This begs the question, "If I am living for God only out of obligation, am I really loving Him?" Furthermore, "If I am living for God only so that I can get something out of Him, am I really loving Him?"

Think about it: While Jesus carried His cross up to the place where He would soon be crucified, He was engaged with the people surrounding Him. They spit on Him, cursed Him, and beat Him. He still died for them.

Romans 5:8 says, "...but God shows His love for us in that while we were still sinners, Christ died for us." As Jesus hung on the cross and took on the sins of the world—past, present, and future—He knew that millions of the people for whom He was dying would ultimately deny Him.

Jesus didn't die so that we *would* love Him back; He died so that we *could* love Him back.

This is important. Before Jesus, it was near impossible to have an intimate relationship with God. Jesus made a way for us to love God intimately within the context of relationship with Him.

Love doesn't give to get something in return; it just gives.

> Love is patient and kind; love does not envy or boast; it is not arrogant or rude. It does not insist on its own way; it is not irritable or resentful; it does not rejoice at wrongdoing, but rejoices with the truth. Love bears all things, believes all things, hopes all things, endures all things.
> *1 Corinthians 14:4-7*

I've encountered God's love in more ways than one.

Here's what I can tell you: His love is deep. It doesn't end. His love is transformative and wild and great!

In Chapter 9, I told you about our once-a-week endeavor with *Love Ambush* when I was in college. In addition to that, my friends and I would go out once a month with the sole purpose of evangelism and praying for people. My friend Josh named the endeavor *Project LOT* (which stood for "Least Of These"). Our mission was to love Jesus by loving the people who were in need.[3]

I had just purchased quite a few birthday party favors for my RA, Ben's, upcoming birthday. Before we left for Jackson, I heard the subtle voice of the Holy Spirit say to me, *Take the party stuff with you. I want to throw a birthday party.*

I wasn't sure the feeling was God, but I grabbed the stuff anyway. We jumped in the car and started off.

As we came toward the local grocery store, I heard that inner voice again: *Buy some cupcakes.* I was a bit hesitant. I told my friends in the car that I had to run a quick errand. I didn't want them to know why. I was afraid there wouldn't be a birthday, and I would've

3 – Jesus said that whatever we do for the "least of these brothers of Mine," we actually did to Him. Check out Matthew 25:31-46 to understand this in context.

prepared for nothing.

I walked in the grocery store and couldn't find any cupcakes. I said, "God, there aren't any cupcakes; only cookies."

He answered, *Cookies are fine.*

Now I was really certain there wouldn't be a birthday. Surly God wasn't speaking to me. God knows everything. If it was really God speaking to me, I reasoned, He would have known there were no cupcakes at the store! I knew I had to be making it up in my head.

Regardless, I bought the cookies out of insecure, blind, teeny-tiny faith.

We reached our first stop, the homeless shelter. We went in and started hanging out with the people there. It was always a good time. Before we started the dinner, I stood up and said, "Is it anybody's birthday?"

I swear I could hear the crickets in the room not just chirp but laugh at me.

I went outside and asked around, yelling at the top of my lungs at people on the street.

It was not one person's birthday!

Surly probability would bail me out! But no one seemed to have a birthday.

Our next and final stop was at a small apartment house. It had about fifteen tenants and was notorious for drug use and prostitution. We knew the owner, and he said we could come and have a worship service in the foyer.

We walked in. I didn't even bring the birthday stuff in from the car. As everyone gathered around, I asked once more if there was anyone present who had a birthday. I said, "God wants to throw a birthday party tonight! Whose birthday is it?"

Once again, the room was silent.

Earlier that day, my friend Steven felt like God wanted him to pray for a lady wearing a pink shirt. Sure enough, there was a lady in a pink shirt standing next to the staircase. He and a few girls from our ministry team went over to pray.
After they prayed, the lady was so moved that she told us she needed to get her friend.

As her friend came downstairs to the foyer, the lady in the pink shirt walked over to talk to us. She announced, "It was her birthday a few days ago. She never got a party."

I did hear from God!

I ran to my car and grabbed the party gear and cookies! I was so excited, I ran across the street and bought some additional gifts at a store. We passed out the favors and all sang happy birthday!

She was blown away. This lady was most likely trapped in human trafficking. She felt forgotten and alone. But God loved her so much that He had a random guy like me buy birthday party supplies and cookies (her favorite kind too!) so she could know that her Father did not forget her birthday.

She requested we sing her favorite childhood song, "Awesome God" by Rich Mullins. We all joined together and witnessed this brothel and drug den become a place of worship!

The drug addict, prostitute, gambler, drunk, ex-convict, and several college students all joined hands and worshiped the God of love.

This love is unlike any other. This love—God's love—is ours to freely receive and freely give. God's love goes the extra mile to show all of us the depth and goodness of His heart.

Love doesn't give to get something in return. It just gives. A good test to see if you are truly loving people and God is to do something that no one will know about—something for which you will not receive anything in return.

I know that idea may seem a little hypocritical considering I've been sharing personal stories throughout this entire book. Some stories are meant to be testimonies. Others are meant to be a test of our sincerity and humility, and those stories should be well-guarded.

Remember my Walmart story from Chapter Three? Immediately after, I felt God challenge me to keep it a secret. Apart from my best friend, I didn't tell anyone for two years until I felt God wanted me to share it one day in a sermon.

There will always be things you do that others know about, but everyone needs God-adventures that are only between them and the Lord.

Go worship God in your room with the door closed for an hour, and don't tell anyone.

Go feed the poor, and don't let anyone see.

Go give to missionaries, and don't let anyone know.

Again, I'm not saying that you need to do everything in secret. It's ok to worship in church when everyone is watching. And it's ok to give to people when others are around. But if you want to test your motives, try being secretive with your sacrifice.

> Thus, when you give to the needy, sound no trumpet before you, as the hypocrites do in the synagogues and in the streets, that they may be praised by others. Truly, I say to you, they have received their reward. But when you give to the needy, do not let your left hand know what your right hand is doing, so that your giving may be in secret. And your Father who sees in secret will reward you.
>
> *Matthew 6:2-4*

Jesus loved without expecting or requiring anything in return. He didn't do it for attention. He loves us—people who really don't have much to offer back. Jesus died for us so that we can have the chance to live with Him forever. He took away our sin so that we could step into freedom.

Jesus loves.

You want to be a man? **Love.**

Conclusion

These aren't the only manly attributes Jesus portrayed. There are plenty more things Jesus did during His time on earth that set the example of how a man of God should act.

Don't stop here.

Dig deep into Scripture. Search for the truth about how Jesus lived.

Place yourself in the narrative of the Bible. After all, until Jesus returns, establishes His throne here, and we see every biblical prophecy fulfilled, we are still living in Bible times. The story is not over.

What story will God write about you? Many men of
God have gone before you. Many have followed Jesus
and known Him. Many have seen their nations, cities,
churches, schools, workplaces, and homes changed by
the power of God at work in them.

The same power that raised Jesus from the dead lives
in you! (See Romans 8:11.) Go and walk in that
power. Walk in your identity as a man of God.

I was hired as a Children's Pastor at a good-sized,
reputable church when I was only 19. I did not let my
age be a reason for issue. I had to hold myself to a
higher standard and step up into my calling.

First Timothy 4:12 says, "Don't let anyone look down
on you because you are young, but set an example for
the believers in speech, in conduct, in love, in faith
and in purity."

You might make mistakes.

You might do stupid things.

I'll even go as far as to say you will *probably* do stupid
things.

Just get up, dust yourself off and keep moving
forward. Men of God can make mistakes. But the
difference from the world is this: Men of God don't

allow their mistakes to define them; they allow Jesus' success to define them.

Now, I need to tie up one loose-end. I've been preaching about being a man of God and how Jesus models what a real man should be. Jesus modeled humility, work ethic, courage, wisdom, gentleness, confidence, strength, joy, compassion, power, and love. We need to follow in His footsteps and live as He did if we want to be the manliest men of God we can be. But there is one question I did neglect to answer—possibly the reason you are reading this book (though I hope not):

Did Jesus *really* have a beard?

Umm… I don't know for sure. No one does.

Believe it or not, there is a lot of debate over that topic. Jesus is depicted by the Catholic Church to have a beard, most likely due to the image on the Shroud of Turin and art passed down through the years. Though many people don't believe that is sufficient, undeniable evidence.

Jewish culture at the time would certainly suggest that Jesus would have worn a beard, or at least not shaven His sideburns (which would have resulted in some seriously thick mutton chops).

There is a prophetic reference to Jesus' beard in Isaiah 50:6, where it is said that Jesus would offer Himself to be beaten and mocked, and they would "pluck out" His beard.

Still—although the disciples recorded the history, they did not have a camera to take a selfie with Jesus.

I personally believe Jesus had a thick, dark beard on His face and a beautifully lush mustache above his upper lip.

Bearded or not, He was a manly man.

But for those of you who aren't satisfied with my answer, I will pose to you a question of my own that may satisfy your curiosity:

How many licks does it take to get to the Tootsie Roll center of Tootsie Pop?

The answer to your question is the same… The world may never know.

Amen.

Discussion Questions

If you happen to go through this book as a group, the following questions will help get the ball rolling with discussion. Take time to think beyond simple answers, feel free to debate ideas, and use your current knowledge of Scripture to help settle disagreements. Allow room for creativity and questions, and take time at the end of each discussion to pray for each other.

1 Humility

- What is humility?

- Who is a man of God you know who sets a good example in humility? Describe him.

- In what ways are you humble?

- In what ways are you not humble?

- How can you strive to become more humble?

2 Work Ethic

☖ What is work ethic?

☖ Do you have a strong work ethic? How do you know?

☖ Work Ethic is often defined as striving for excellence. If that is true, how can we strive for excellence in our lives?

☖ How can we strive for excellence in the arts, relationships, academics, athletics, or holiness?

☖ What things keep us from striving for excellence?

3 Courage

☖ What is Courage?

☖ Is Courage dependent on the existence of fear? Why or why not?

☖ Share a story about a time when you were courageous.

☖ What does it feel like to be courageous?

☖ How can we become courageous?

4 Wisdom

O   What is wisdom?

O   How do we identify the difference between what is wise and what is foolish?

O   How can we be wise and still have fun?

O   Who is someone you would consider wise? Describe the evidence and indicators in that person's life that show wisdom.

5 Gentleness

O   What is gentleness?

O   In what ways is gentleness similar to self control?

O   Was Jesus always gentle?

O   Are there justifiable times to be violent?

O   Can you be strong and courageous and gentle at the same time?

6 Confidence

🕭 What is confidence?

🕭 What attributes of a relationship with God lead to healthy confidence?

🕭 How can we become more confident in our understanding of how God sees us?

🕭 How does our understanding of God shape our confidence?

🕭 How does our identity shape our confidence?

🕭 How does confidence impact our prayers?

7 Strength

🕭 What is strength?

🕭 In what ways is strength more than physical?

🕭 Who is someone you consider strong? Explain.

🕭 How do difficult situations make us stronger?

🕭 How have you experienced God's strength?

8 Joy

- What is joy?

- Do you consider yourself a joyful person? Why or why not?

- How can we have joy in tough times?

- What is the difference between joy and happiness?

- Is God joyful? Is He in a good mood? Can you think of any Scriptures to support your answer?

9 Compassion

- What is compassion?

- Who do you feel compassion for?

- Have you ever asked God to allow you to experience His compassion? If so, what happened? Did anything change in you?

- How can we live aware of so much hurt in the world without losing our joy?

- How was Jesus compassionate?

10 Power

Q What is power?

Q What are we to do with the power God gives?

Q How did the Jesus walk in the power of the Holy Spirit?

Q How did the disciples walk in the power of the Holy Spirit?

Q What holds us back from living lives infused with the power of the Holy Spirit?

Q Name an area of your life in which you need the power of the Holy Spirit?

11 Love

Q What is love?

Q Are there different types of love?

Q How do we love others like Jesus did?

Q How do we selflessly love others without neglecting ourselves?

Q Is it wrong to say "no" to someone in need?

Q Who do you consider to be a man of God who loves God, others, and himself well?

About the Author

Casey Noce is a pastor on staff at Bethany Assembly of God, a high school teacher, and a coach in Adrian, Michigan. He has a desire to see young men equipped with the know-how they need to live like Jesus.

Casey is passionate about mentorship. This book encapsulates his heart to "brother" younger men of God.

Casey is also the author of *30 – Peace & Joy*, a 30-day devotional of "One-minute Messages for Middle School Men," available through Supernatural Truth Productions (www.SupernaturalTruth.com).

JESUS HAD A BEARD ◐ — CASEY NOCE

122

Know someone younger than you who you know could use some encouragement? Start being a mentor today, and buy them a copy of Casey's other book.

This powerful devotional gives the junior high student daily opportunities to connect with God and start their day off right. And since no teenager wants to roll out of bed until the last possible moment, we made each lesson so it can be read in only about one minute.

30 contains 30 "one-minute messages for middle school men" about living a life of peace and joy. Each lesson contains a scripture, a paraphrase of that verse, a short teaching by Casey Noce, and a prayer. Room is given with each lesson for journaling if desired. (128 pages)

Available at SupernaturalTruth.com or anywhere books are sold.

Please consider sharing this book with a friend and writing a review on Amazon.com.

Additional copies available at
www.SupernaturalTruth.com

Made in the USA
San Bernardino, CA
18 March 2017